PAPERCRAFTS
FOR
CHRISTMAS

MAKING CARDS AND DECORATIONS

PAPERCRAFTS
FOR
CHRISTMAS

MAKING CARDS AND DECORATIONS
JUDY BALCHIN AND POLLY PINDER

SEARCH PRESS

First published in Great Britain 2008

Search Press Limited
Wellwood, North Farm Road,
Tunbridge Wells, Kent TN2 3DR

Based on the following books published by Search Press:
Making Christmas Cards by Judy Balchin (2005)
Making Christmas Tree Decorations by Judy Balchin (2006)
Making Christmas Table Decorations by Polly Pinder (2006)

Text copyright © Judy Balchin, Polly Pinder

Photographs by Storm Studios and Roddy Paine
Photographic Studios

Photographs and design copyright © Search Press 2008

ISBN-13: 978-1-84448-317-4

Suppliers
If you have any difficulty obtaining any of the materials and
equipment mentioned in this book, then please visit the Search
Press website for details of suppliers:
www.searchpress.com

Publisher's note
All the step-by-step photographs in this book feature the
authors, Judy Balchin and Polly Pinder, demonstrating
papercraft techniques. No models have been used.

Printed in China

Contents

Making Christmas Cards

by Judy Balchin

If, like me, you love Christmas, then this is definitely the book for you. Handmade Christmas cards are fun to make and a joy to receive. The desire to express greetings at Christmas is universal. It is a time to tell those around you just how special they are and what could be more perfect than to make them a handcrafted card.

The sending of a seasonal message goes back a long way, dating as far back as pagan times when good luck charms were exchanged at the Winter Solstice. Greetings cards have been a huge part of our Christmas celebrations for over a hundred and fifty years. In fact, the first printed Christmas card was created in 1843 by Sir Henry Cole, director of London's Victoria and Albert Museum.

These days, printed cards can be bought inexpensively and are sent in their millions all over the world. In this fast world of mass production, isn't it lovely to receive something just that little bit different, made with care and sent with love?

Many of you crafters will have found that your creative talents have guided you through lots of different crafts and this is where this section will help you. Whether it be stitching and embossing, glass or silk painting or just having fun with stickers or wire and beads, there is something for everyone within these pages. You are given simple projects to follow and then shown further card ideas to inspire you. My hope is for you to use this section as a launching pad for your own designs, and for those of you who say that you can't draw – don't worry, patterns are provided for every card.

Good luck on your festive journey. Enjoy the adventure and, most importantly, have fun!

Judy

An array of beautiful handmade cards.

Basic materials

You will not need all of the equipment and materials shown on these pages to start your projects. Each individual project provides you with a specific list of requirements for you to look at before you begin.

Pencil Use this to trace designs or to draw them on to card.

Ruler For measuring card, drawing straight lines and, with scissors, to score a fold in a card.

Felt tip pen Useful for tracing around a pattern on to felt or fabric.

Paintbrushes Use a larger brush for applying silk paint to silk (see Seasonal Silk Tree). A smaller paintbrush is used for glass painting (see Festive Fairy) and the detailed painting of the outline sticker (see Bethlehem Sticker Scene).

Scalpel Lift outline stickers with the tip of a scalpel. Use with a **cutting mat** to trim card and paper to the required size.

Scissors Large scissors are used to cut paper, silk and felt. Use small sharp scissors to cut around a painted acetate design (see Festive Fairy) and to score card.

Hole punch Useful for making holes in gift tags for threading with ribbon.

Masking tape Use this for securing patterns and acetate when glass painting (see Festive Fairy). Also use to secure a design behind an aperture card (see Embossed Motifs).

Tracing paper Use this to trace your patterns from the book if a photocopier is not available.

Newspaper Cover your work surface with newspaper when using spray glue. Used for embossing (see Embossed Motifs).

Spray glue For securing papers and silk to card.

Strong glue Such as PVA or superglue. Use this to secure gems, sequins and decorations to a card.

3D foam squares These are used to attach a design panel to a card to give a raised three-dimensional effect. They are also used to keep wire in place when wrapped round a shaped card decoration (see Wire & Bead Star).

General materials for card making

A huge choice of backing card and papers is available nowadays from art and craft shops. This selection includes handmade paper, assorted coloured cards, holographic, mirror and pearlised card, corrugated card, webbing and felt.

Card decorations

Ribbons, coloured cottons, beads, sequins, buttons, gems and glitter glue can all be used to enhance your cards.

Paints

Silk, glass and watercolour paints are used in creating some of the cards in this book. Each project provides you with a specific list of paints and colours.

STITCHED STOCKING

Stitching gives this first project that really cosy 'handmade' look. The simple felt stocking is decorated with embroidered stars and glass beads. Remember to keep the basic shape as simple as possible when working in this way, then you can really go to town on the decorative stitching and beadwork. Felt is readily available and comes in a wonderful array of colours. Using contrasting cotton for the stitching and embroidery will make sure that your creation takes pride of place on any mantelpiece at Christmas.

You will need:

Red felt, 7 x 12cm
(2¾ x 4¾in)

Pink felt, 3 x 6cm
(1¼ x 2½in)

Pink handmade paper,
9 x 14cm (3½ x 5½in)

Burgundy card,
9 x 14cm (3½ x 5½in)

Gold card, 15 x 20cm
(6 x 7¾in)

Pink and blue
embroidery cottons

Gold glitter glue

Needle

Small blue beads

Felt tip pen

Scissors

Spray glue

Mouse mat

Ruler

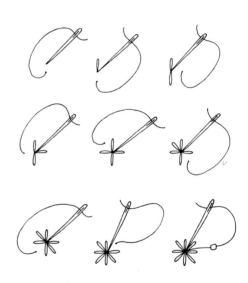

Follow this diagram to create the stitches used on the stocking.

Tip

Felt is perfect for stitching as it does not fray. If you haven't got any, you can stitch on to coloured card.

The template for the Stitched Stocking card.

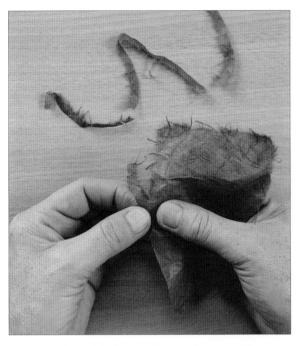

1. Tear a 5mm (¼in) strip from each edge of the rectangle of handmade paper.

2. Spray the back with spray glue and press it on to the middle of the piece of burgundy card.

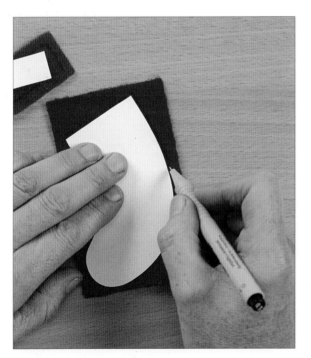

3. Photocopy the stocking patterns and cut them out. Lay the paper patterns on to the red felt and draw round the shapes with the felt tip pen.

4. Cut them out.

5. Using strong glue, glue the small rectangular 'cuff' to the top of the stocking.

6. Use the felt tip pen to draw random spots over the stocking as a guide to your embroidery.

7. Using three strands of pink embroidery cotton, thread your needle and knot the end of the thread. Using the diagram on page 10 to help you, sew one star at the top of the stocking.

8. Thread a bead and then push your needle back through the centre of the star. Continue in this way, sewing stars down the felt stocking.

9. Glue the embroidered stocking to the middle of the handmade paper.

10. Lay the panel on a mouse mat. Using your needle, prick stitch holes in the pink paper around the edge of the stocking.

11. Thread your needle with blue embroidery cotton, knot the end and stitch round the stocking.

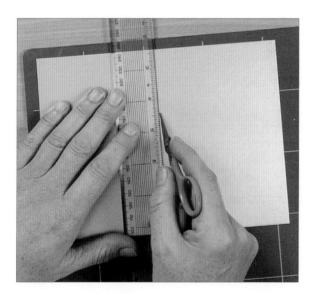

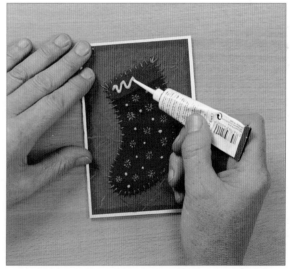

12. Score and fold the gold card down the middle.

13. Glue your stocking panel to the front of the gold card. Add dots of gold glitter glue between the stars. Finally, run a wavy line of glitter glue along the 'cuff' and leave to dry.

The finished Stitched Stocking card.

*Stitching, beads, glitter glue, felt and handmade paper
can be used to make a variety of lovely cards.*

EMBOSSED MOTIFS

You will need:

Silver embossing foil,
10 x 11cm (4 x 4¼in)

Gold card, 6 x 13cm
(2½ x 5in)

Cream card, 21 x 24cm
(8¼ x 9½in)

Gold and silver
ribbons, various widths

Gold star decoration

Ballpoint pen

Pencil and ruler

Scalpel

Cutting mat

Scissors

Newspaper

Piece of scrap paper

Strong glue

Spray glue

Masking tape

And now for something a little more sophisticated.
The combination of metal foil and ribbons
enclosed in a cream surround gives a crisp, modern feel
to this card. Embossing the simple motifs is not difficult but is very
effective when combined with the glitzy rows of ribbon and gold card.
You are provided with instructions for making the aperture card.
Measure and cut it out carefully to achieve a truly professional finish.

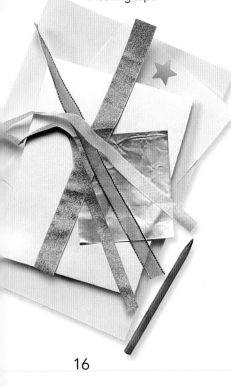

*The embossing
patterns.*

*Follow these
measurements to
create the card.*

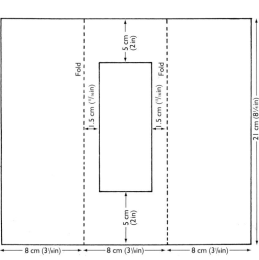

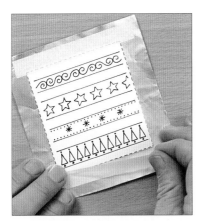

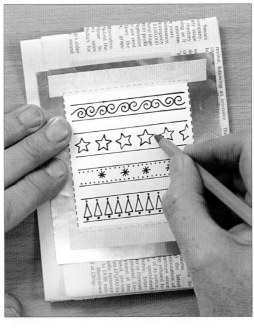

Tip

A ballpoint pen is the perfect tool for creating the embossed lines for this card.

1. Photocopy the embossing pattern and cut it out. Lay the foil face down on your work surface, then tape your pattern on top with some masking tape.

2. Fold up some newspaper and put the foil and the pattern on top. Trace over the pattern with a ballpoint pen.

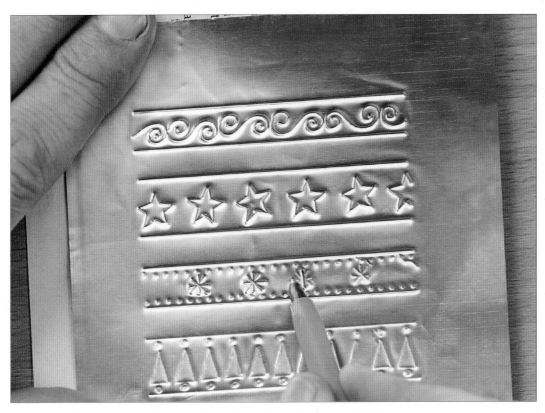

3. Remove the pattern and go over the embossed lines to deepen them.

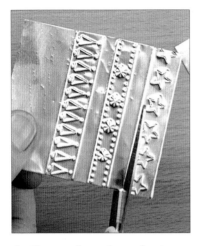

4. Cut out the embossed strips.

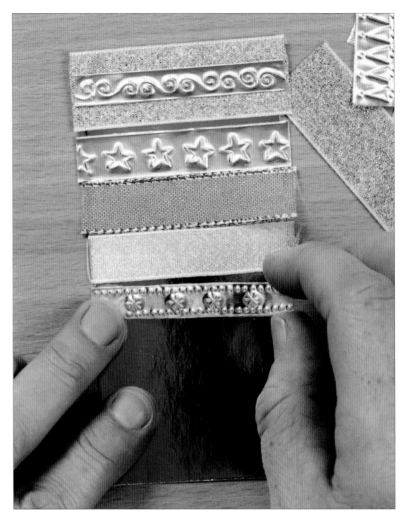

5. Cut some lengths of ribbon the same length as the foil strips. Use the strong glue to glue the strips of foil and the ribbon to the gold card, leaving some spaces so that the gold card can be seen between the strips.

6. Turn the panel over and trim off the overhanging foil and ribbon.

7. Using the diagram on page 16 to help you, measure and pencil in the fold lines and aperture on the cream card. Score the folds with scissors and cut out the aperture.

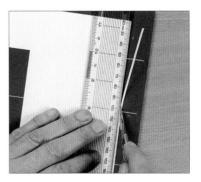

8. Cut a 2mm ($^1/_{16}$in) strip from the left-hand edge of the card.

9. Tape your decorated panel face down behind the aperture with strips of masking tape.

10. Cover the right-hand third of your cream card with a piece of scrap paper. Spray the remaining card with spray glue.

11. Fold the left-hand flap over and press to secure.

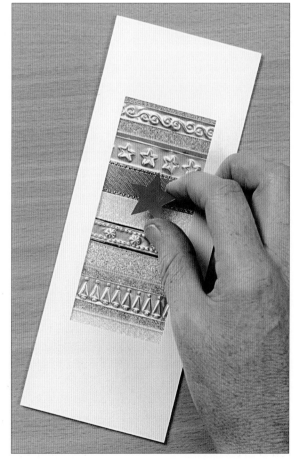

12. Turn the card over and glue a gold star to the middle of your decorated panel.

The finished Embossed Motifs card.

You can create lots of different shapes and patterns for cards with embossing.

SEASONAL SILK TREE

You will need:

Habotai silk, 12 x 18cm
(4¾ x 7in)

Emerald green and
turquoise silk paints

Tube of gold gutta

Thick white card,
5.5 x 12cm
(2¼ x 4¾in)

Blue card, 15 x 18cm
(6 x 7in)

Gold card, 6 x 12.5cm
(2½ x 5in)

Red glitter glue

Star decoration

Masking tape

Paintbrush

Scissors

Pencil

Sheet of polythene

Newspaper

Spray glue

Iron

If you love messing about with paints, then this project is definitely for you. Colouring the silk is great fun and no two cards will ever be the same with this technique. The simple tree design is piped over the coloured silk with gold gutta. The addition of a glittery pot, baubles and a shining star will ensure that your friends will be delighted to display this mini masterpiece.

The template for the Seasonal Silk Tree card.

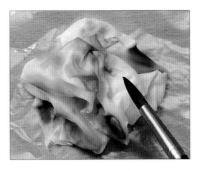

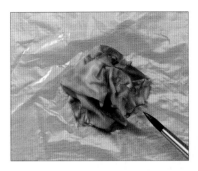

1. Immerse the piece of silk in water and squeeze out the excess. Lay the crumpled wet silk on the sheet of polythene.

2. Dot on emerald silk paint with a paintbrush.

3. Repeat with the turquoise silk paint.

4. Turn the crumpled silk over and repeat, making sure that the silk is completely coloured. Leave to dry.

Tip

The wet silk can be dried with a hair dryer. Place it under a sieve or colander while drying to prevent it from blowing away.

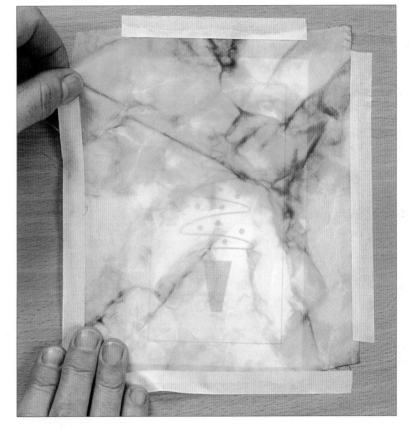

5. Iron the silk. Photocopy the pattern, cut around it and lay it on your work surface. Spread the silk out and, using masking tape, tape it down over the pattern, making sure it is stretched taut.

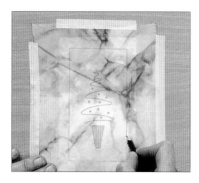

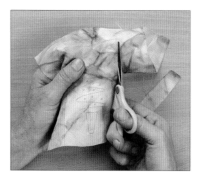

6. Trace the pattern with a pencil. Do not trace the star.

7. Remove the masking tape and cut out the silk rectangle. Lay it on some newspaper and spray the back of the silk lightly with spray glue.

8. Lay the card rectangle in the middle of the silk and cut away the corners as shown.

9. Fold the silk over the edges as shown, making sure they stick securely.

10. Score and fold the blue card down the middle. Glue the gold card to the front of the blue card.

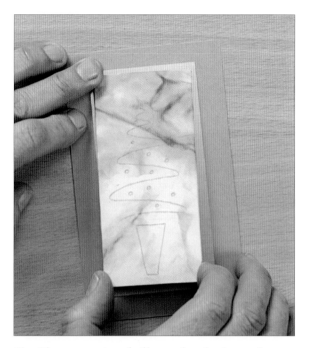

11. Glue your painted silk panel to the front of the card.

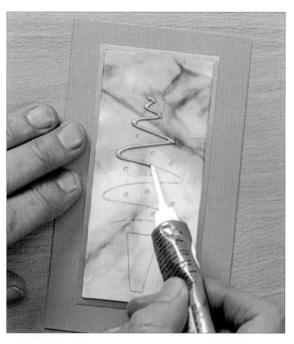

12. Use the tube of gutta to pipe in the wavy line of the Christmas tree.

13. Add baubles and a plant pot using glitter glue.

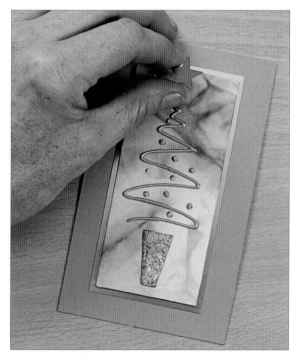

14. Glue the star decoration just above the tree and leave to dry.

The finished Seasonal Silk Tree card.

Experiment with various paint colours to achieve different effects.

WIRE & BEAD STAR

You will need:

Pearl lilac card,
10.5 x 21cm
(4¼ x 8¼in) and a
8.5cm (3½in) square

Pink handmade paper,
5.5 x 9cm (2¼ x 3½in)

Iridescent star
decoration

1 metre of silver wire

Pink beads

3D foam squares

Spray glue

Scissors

Scalpel

Cutting mat

Ruler

If, like me, you hoard crafty bits and bobs gathered here and there as you trawl the craft shops, then you will definitely want to have a go at this project. With a little wire, card, handmade paper and some beads, you can create a very stylish card indeed. Colour schemes are important. The bright pink beads combine well with the vibrant handmade paper and the more subtle pearlised lilac card. The iridescent star is ready made, but can easily be reproduced with the template below.

The template for the star.

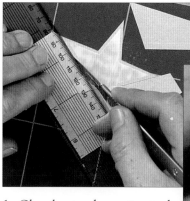

1. Glue the star decoration to the square of lilac card. Use a ruler and scalpel to cut around the edge so that it has a 2mm (¹⁄₁₆in) border of lilac card all around the star.

2. Press 3D foam squares to the back of the star and remove the backing papers.

3. Attach one end of the wire on to the back of the 3D foam squares.

4. Bring the wire round to the front and thread on a few beads.

Tip
Lay your small beads ready for threading on a piece of cloth to prevent them from rolling away.

5. Take the wire around to the back again.

6. Continue in this way until you have wrapped the wire around five times to create an inner beaded star shape.

7. Press the wire on to the 3D foam squares and trim the end to neaten.

8. Cut a 3D foam square to make five small squares and add to each point of the star. Put to one side.

10. Glue the handmade paper to the left-hand side of the front of the card.

9. Tear a 5mm (¼in) strip from the right-hand edge of the handmade paper.

11. Press the finished star decoration on to the front of the lilac card base, lining up the top of the star with the edge of the torn handmade paper.

The finished Wire & Bead Star card.

Opposite: The wire can be curled to create a ribbon effect on gifts and trailing stars.

FESTIVE FAIRY

You will need:

Acetate, 9 x 14cm (3½ x 5½in)

Thick white card, 12 x 16cm (4¾ x 6¼in)

Holographic card, 8 x 12.5cm (3¼ x 5in)

Red shiny card, 18 x 13.5cm (7 x 5¼in)

Glass paints: clear, red, orange, yellow, green, turquoise

Tube of black outliner

Red gems

Silver star decorations

Paintbrush

Palette

Small scissors

Strong glue

Masking tape

Spray glue

Time to get out those glass paints and have some fun. Take a little time to practise using the outliner tube on paper first. Practice makes perfect as they say and the aim is to achieve an even, unbroken line. Painting your fairy is great fun but you may want to dilute some of the more dense paints with clear glass paint to lighten the colour, as light will not be shining through the design. Backing the painted acetate design with holographic card adds a real sparkle to your festive friend!

The template for the Festive Fairy card.

1. Photocopy the pattern, cut around it and tape it to the piece of thick white card. Tape the acetate over the pattern.

2. Use the tube of outliner to outline the design. Leave to dry.

3. Lift up the acetate and remove the pattern underneath. Retape the acetate to the white card.

4. Paint the fairy's hair and wings with yellow paint.

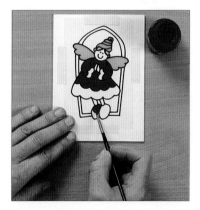

5. Paint the dress and shoes in red.

Tip

Apply the paint generously so that it settles flat within the outlined area.

6. Paint the cuffs and dress hem in orange.

7. Mix some clear glass paint and a spot of orange for the skin areas.

8. Mix a pale turquoise for the background.

9. Paint the border in green. Leave to dry.

10. Cut around the design carefully.

11. Spray the back of the acetate with spray glue and stick the acetate fairy to the holographic card.

12. Fold the red card and glue the fairy design to the front.

13. Glue some red gems to the fairy's dress hem.

14. Add some silver stars to the turquoise background.

The finished Festive Fairy card.

Try adding beads, jewels and stickers to create fun details on your cards.

BETHLEHEM STICKER SCENE

You will need:

Silver Bethlehem outline sticker

Deckle edged cream card blank, 14.5cm (5¾in) square

Watercolour paper, 12cm (4¾in) square

White glitter webbing, 12cm (4¾in) square

Silver mirror card, 9cm (3½in) square

Silk paints: yellow, raspberry, cyan, turquoise and iris

Pink ribbon, 8cm (3¼in)

Paintbrush

Palette

Spray glue

Strong glue

3D foam squares

Scalpel

Outline stickers really do take all the hard work out of card making. Just peel them off, stick them down and then decorate them with paints. Vibrant silk paints are used to paint this Bethlehem scene, giving it a rich glow; just right for Christmas. Alternatively, watercolours can be used. Colours can be painted flat or blended within each section to give the design more depth. Some of the stars from the sticker sheet are used to decorate the co-ordinating ribbon hanging from the main design.

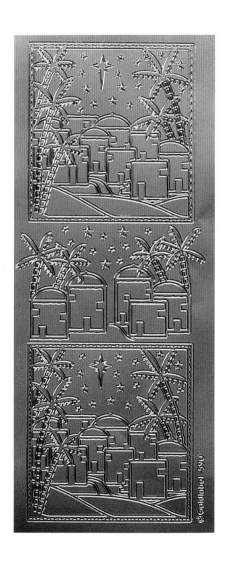

The Bethlehem outline sticker.

1. Use a scalpel to peel the sticker away from the backing sheet. Leave it to rest for a minute to regain its shape. Press it on to the watercolour paper.

2. Paint each section with water before applying the paint. This makes it easier to blend the colours.

3. Paint the hills in yellow and, while the paint is still wet, add a little raspberry and blend it in for shading.

4. Paint the paths, steps and buildings with iris, turquoise and cyan. Paints can be mixed together on a palette or diluted with water to create different hues and shades.

5. For the palm tree trunks, mix yellow and raspberry to create a dark orange colour.

6. Paint the upper part of the sky with cyan. While the paint is still wet, fill in the lower half with raspberry.

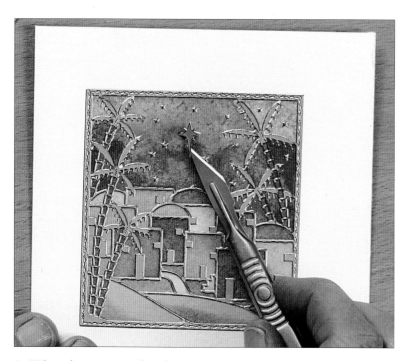

7. When dry, press small outline stars on to the sky area and trim around the design.

8. Glue the piece of ribbon to the back of the design.

10. Glue the square of mirror card on top of the webbing.

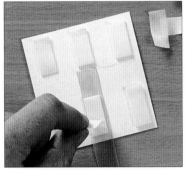

11. Apply some 3D foam squares on to the back of your design and remove the backing papers.

9. Spray glue the glitter webbing and press it on to the front of the card blank.

12. Press the design on to the mirror card.

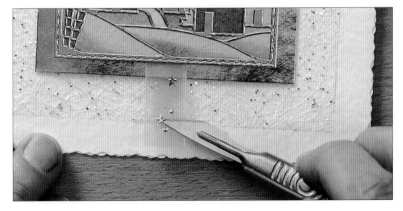

13. Press some small sticky stars on to the tail of ribbon.

The finished Bethlehem Sticker Scene card.

Opposite: There are various outline stickers available to try on your cards.

Templates

Stitched Stocking variations (see page 15)

These templates are shown full size.

Embossed Motifs variations (see page 21)

These templates are shown full size.

Seasonal Silk Tree variations (see page 27)

These templates are shown full size.

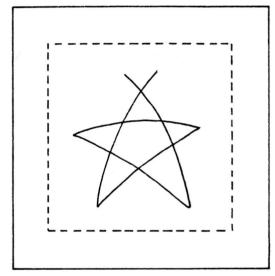

Wire & Bead Star variations (see page 33)

These templates are shown half size. You will need to enlarge them 100% on a photocopier.

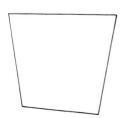

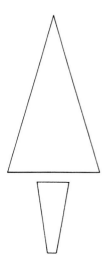

Festive Fairy variations (see page 39)

These templates are shown half size. You will need to enlarge them 100% on a photocopier.

Twinkling Tree
Have fun sewing assorted sequins and beads to a felt Christmas tree.

Wire & Jewel Snowflakes

Cool colours, snowflake decorations and silver wire and beads have been used to create a crisp, modern card.

Making Christmas Tree Decorations

by Judy Balchin

Ah Christmas... It is my favourite time of year, so you can imagine what fun I've had making all these Christmas tree decorations. Christmas is a very special time spent with family and friends and preparations are usually in full swing well before the big day. Decorating the house is wonderful, but perhaps the crowning glory to any Christmas scene is the Christmas tree twinkling away.

It was the husband of Queen Victoria, Prince Albert, who introduced the Christmas tree to this country in 1841, when he decorated the first tree at Windsor Castle with sweets, candles, gingerbread and fruit. In the 1850s, Charles Dickens describes a Christmas tree decorated with costume jewellery, toy guns, miniature furniture, musical instruments, fruits and sweets. It must have been magnificent to behold! By 1890 Christmas decorations were being imported from Germany. Nowadays, inexpensive shop-bought decorations are available everywhere. They are so much part of our Christmas experience that we can hardly imagine the time when they all had to be home-made. Now we have the choice, and hopefully by the time you have looked through the pages of this section, you will be inspired to have a go at making your own.

I have spent many hours in a haze of glitter and glue trying to give you a varied choice of decorations. Folk art garlands, funky angels, decorative crackers, festive tree present labels, sparkling stars and glitzy gift boxes are all waiting to be made and displayed on the big day.

So gather your family and a few friends, settle round that kitchen table and have fun creating decorations for your own Christmas tree this year.

Judy

This picture shows just a small selection of the Christmas tree decorations in this section. All the decorations are inexpensive and fun to make.

Basic materials

You will not need all the materials shown here to start your projects. Each individual project has its own list of specific requirements.

General materials

A huge and wonderful range of card and backing papers are available in art and craft shops. This selection includes handmade papers, assorted coloured card and backing papers, metallic, pearlised, corrugated and holographic card and embossing foils. Papier-mâché blanks are available from art and craft shops in a wide variety of shapes and sizes.

Paints and inks

Acrylic paints are easily available from art and craft shops, as are inks. Use acrylic paints to sponge papier-mâché boxes before decorating. Coloured inks are used to paint watercolour paper. Glitter glue is great for bringing a little sparkle to your Christmas tree decorations.

Stamps and embossing powders

Rubber stamps, embossing pads and powders are available from art and craft outlets. Look out for Christmas themed stamps for your decorations. The heating tool is used to melt the embossing powder on to a surface. Take care with the heating tool, as it is extremely hot, and be sure to work on a heatproof surface.

Embellishments

Ribbons, embroidery thread, wire, cord, raffia, fancy yarns, beads, buttons, sequins, craft jewels, mini pegs, paper stars, eyelets, craft stickers – the list goes on. All can be used to enhance your Christmas tree decorations.

Other materials and equipment

Pencil Use this to trace round templates or copy them on to card or paper.

Ruler For measuring card, drawing straight lines and, with the back of a scalpel, to score a fold.

Fine black felt tip pen To draw round the painted star template and to add stitch lines to punched motifs.

Pencil crayon Use this to draw the mouth and cheeks on to the angel cone.

Paintbrushes Use a large brush to apply water and coloured inks to watercolour paper. Use the rounded end of a paintbrush to emboss foil.

Old ballpoint pen Use this for embossing foil.

Palette Squeeze paint on to a palette when using a sponge to decorate an item.

Scalpel Use this to cut card and to score a fold with the back of the scalpel.

Cutting mat Use a cutting mat when cutting card or paper with a scalpel.

Needle Use to thread ribbons, buttons and sequins.

Scissors Trim ribbon and thread with scissors.

Old scissors Use old scissors to cut wire.

Old notepad To use when embossing foils.

Masking tape Use to secure a pattern to foil when embossing.

Spray glue For securing card or paper to surfaces.

Clear glue Use to attach craft jewels and buttons.

Glue line A strong line of glue used to secure the cracker and the angel cone.

Sponge Papier-mâché boxes are sponged with paint to give an even, slightly textured surface.

Hairdryer Use to speed up the drying of paper painted with coloured inks.

Eyelet kit This includes a hammer and mat, and a multipurpose tool for punching holes in card and paper and setting eyelets.

Plastic tubing Use to roll the paper when making a Christmas cracker.

String Use to create the indentations in a Christmas cracker and to string together a garland.

Punches Use to cut paper shapes for decoration.

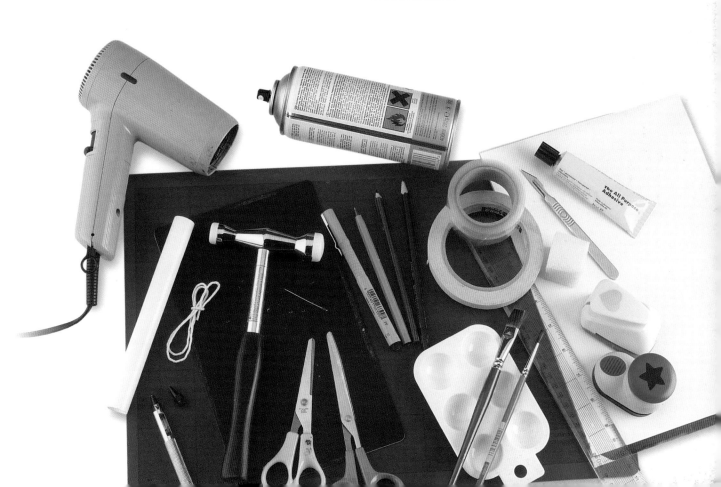

SEASONAL STOCKING GARLAND

You will need:

Red and green handmade papers

Watercolour paper

Fine black felt tip pen

Paper stars

Heart punch

String

Raffia

Mini pegs

Glitter glue

Clear glue

Pencil

Scissors

As a child I can well remember the enjoyment of making brightly coloured paper garlands for the Christmas tree. With a little paper, string, and glitter glue it is amazing what you can come up with! These mini stocking garlands are easy and fun to make. Keep the basic shapes simple as you will be cutting out quite a few to create your garland. The stitching adds a folk art feel and is done quickly and easily with a felt tip pen.

The templates for the Seasonal Stocking Garland project, reproduced at actual size.

1. Photocopy the stocking template and cut it out. Lay it on handmade paper and draw round it with a pencil. Make four stockings of each colour.

2. Cut out the stockings.

3. Punch eight hearts; four of each colour.

4. Use the cuff template to help you make the eight cuffs. Tear 5mm (¼in) from each edge. Glue the cuffs to the tops of the stockings using clear glue.

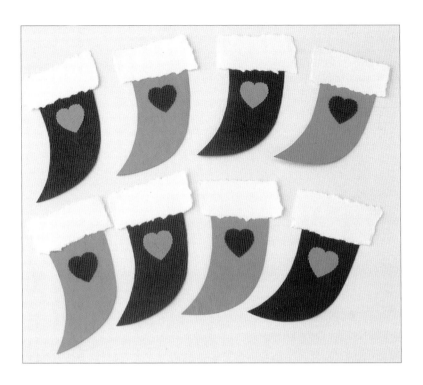

5. Attach the hearts in alternating colours on to the stocking using clear glue.

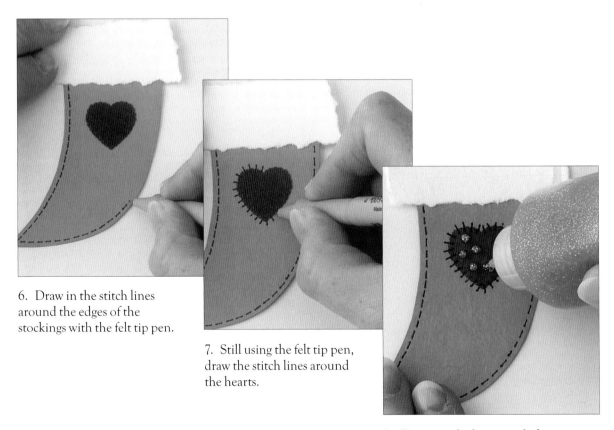

6. Draw in the stitch lines around the edges of the stockings with the felt tip pen.

7. Still using the felt tip pen, draw the stitch lines around the hearts.

8. Decorate the hearts with dots of glitter glue.

9. Run a line of glitter glue down the front of eight mini pegs.

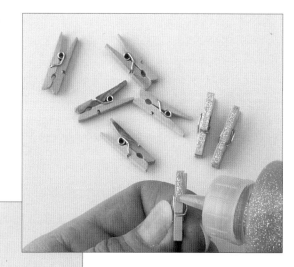

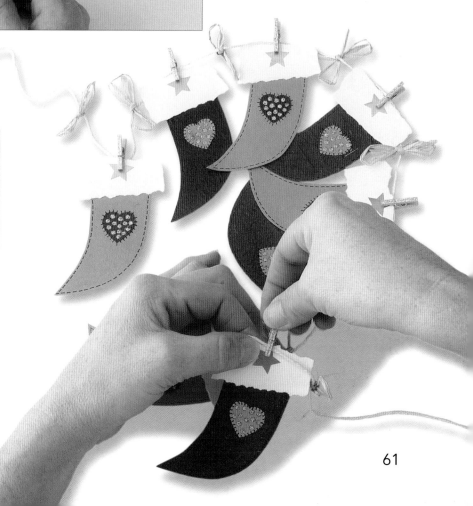

10. Tie small raffia bows down a length of string.

Tip

Traditional colours are used to create this garland. As an alternative, try using more unusual colour combinations for a more modern look.

11. Peg the stockings and a paper star between each bow, with the glittery side of the peg to the front.

61

Seasonal Stocking Garland

This garland is simple to make but very effective when strung across the tree branches.

Simple shapes, textured papers and a little glitter glue are used to create these garlands.

FLIGHTS OF FANCY

You will need

White card, 13 x 18cm (5 x 7in)

Pink card, 4 x 10cm (1½ x 4in)

Iridescent glitter glue

Black felt tip pen

Pink pencil crayon

Silver wire

Pink beads

Pink fancy yarn

Pink embroidery thread

Pencil

Paintbrush

Ruler

Scissors

Scalpel

Cutting mat

Glue line

Clear glue

This basic cone shape gives you great scope for decoration. Have fun creating a host of twinkling angels to fly through the branches of your Christmas tree. Use bright coloured fancy yarns to give them funky hairstyles to match their glitzy robes and beaded feet.

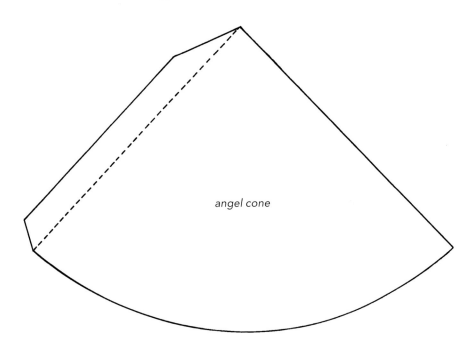

angel cone

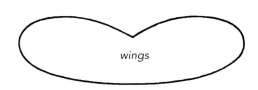

wings

The templates for the Flights of Fancy project, reproduced at three quarters of the actual size. Enlarge them to 133 per cent on a photocopier.

1. Lay the angel template on to the white card, and the wings template on to the pink card. Draw round them and cut them out.

2. Score down the inner line of the angel cone with the back of the scalpel, using the dotted line on the template to help you with positioning.

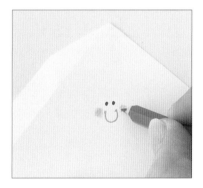

3. Draw in the eyes with a felt tip pen. Draw in the mouth with a pencil crayon and colour in the cheeks.

4. Pipe swirls of glitter glue over the body area of the angel and leave to dry.

Tip

As an alternative, try piping spots, stars or stripes of glitter glue on to the cone.

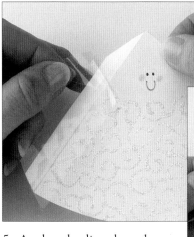

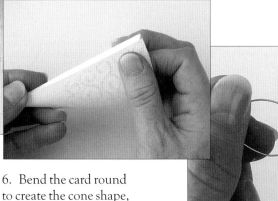

5. Apply a glue line along the tab of the angel cone and peel off the backing paper.

6. Bend the card round to create the cone shape, securing it with the glue line.

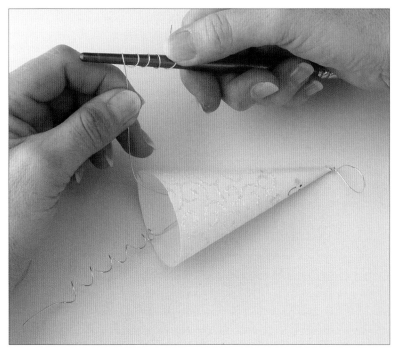

7. Make a loop in the middle of a 60cm (24in) piece of wire. Twist the loop round to form a secure hoop.

8. Poke the ends of the wire down through the top of the cone to create the legs, then bend the hoop over to create the halo.

9. Twist each of the leg wires round the end of a paintbrush to create spirals.

10. Thread a bead on to the end of each spiral. Bend the wires back and twist to secure.

Tip

The angel's hair can be created with coloured wool, pipe cleaners, raffia or string. The choice is yours!

11. Apply clear glue to the top of the cone and wrap with fancy yarn.

12. Use clear glue to attach the wings to the back of the angel.

13. Tie a loop of matching embroidery thread to the wire halo for the hanger.

There is always room for humour and these angels will certainly raise a smile.

*Make a host of different angels by using different coloured yarns for hair
and fancy card for the wings.*

LABELS OF LOVE

You will need:

A5 sheet of red card

Music-themed
backing paper,
6 x 6 cm (2¼ x 2¼in)

Floral backing paper,
6 x 6cm (2¼ x 2¼in)

Gold embossing foil

Ballpoint pen

Paintbrush

Old notepad

Gold star and line
craft stickers

Eyelet kit

Gold eyelet

Gold cord

Clear glue

Spray glue

Pencil

Scissors

Ruler

Scalpel

Cutting mat

Masking tape

Many of us hang small 'tree presents' on the tree at Christmas. These are personal gifts especially for those sharing the festive Christmas celebrations. This decorative label is ideal as it provides you with a small pocket to hold the gift. The pocket is decorated with an embossed initial to personalise the label and make it

The templates for the Labels of Love project, reproduced at three quarters of the actual size. Enlarge them to 133 per cent on a photocopier.

Label

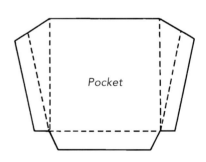

Pocket

1. Cut out a label and pocket
    shape from card using the
    templates to help you.

2. Score the lines on the pocket with the back of the scalpel.

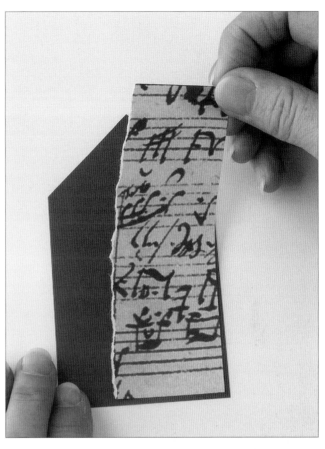

3. Tear a 5mm (¼in) strip from the left-hand side of the music backing paper and spray glue it to the label.

4. Turn the label over and trim off the excess paper.

5. Tear a 5mm (¼in) strip from the right-hand edge of the floral backing and glue it in place.

6. Photocopy the required letter from the alphabet (see pages 94–95 for further templates). Cut round it and tape it to the back of the gold embossing foil.

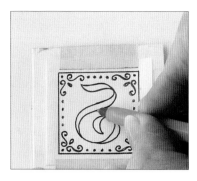

7. Lay the foil on a padded surface. Trace over the design with a ballpoint pen.

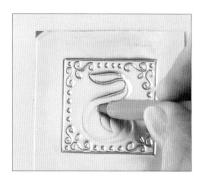

8. Remove the pattern and trace over it once more to deepen the embossed line.

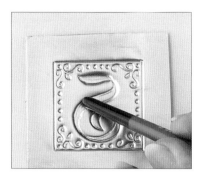

9. Use the rounded end of a paintbrush to emboss the letter.

10. Fold the pocket flaps back. Spread the flaps with clear glue and press the pocket on to the label.

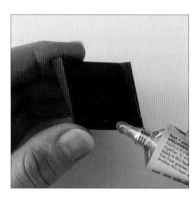

11. Cut out the letter square and glue it to the front of the pocket.

12. Decorate the label with star and line craft stickers.

13. Punch a hole in the top of the label with the hole punch and hammer.

14. Insert an eyelet and hammer the back with the eyelet setter to secure.

15. Thread the hole with cord, creating a half-hitch as shown.

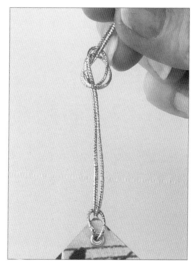

16. Tie the cord in a knot at the top to create the hanger.

17. Wrap a small gift in festive paper and slip it into the pocket.

The embossed gold foil and craft stickers add an extra sparkle to this festive label.

Use bells, craft jewels, craft stickers and assorted backing papers to create labels for all your family and friends.

WHAT A CRACKER!

You will need:

Floral backing paper, 8 x 17cm (3 x 6¾in)

Gold paper, A5

Gold wire

Pink ribbon, 50cm (20in)

Button

Length of plastic tubing, approximate diameter 2cm (¾in)

Glue line

Spray glue

Old scissors

Scalpel

Cutting mat

Ruler and pencil

String

No Christmas tree is complete without a few Christmas crackers. This basic cracker is created using background paper and decorated with gold paper, wire and a button to give a delicate feminine look. You could choose bolder coloured background paper and embellishments to create a more traditional look to your crackers.

The template for the What a Cracker! project, reproduced at actual size.

1. Using the dotted lines on the template to help you with positioning, draw six lines across the back of the background paper.

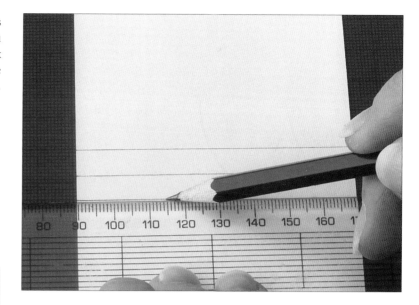

2. With the back of the scalpel, lightly score the six lines on the cracker.

3. Cut slits between the scored lines as shown.

4. Turn the backing paper over and spray glue a 2cm (¾in) wide strip of gold paper across the end of the cracker. Then tear a 5mm (¼in) strip from the end of the cracker.

5. Repeat this process on the other end of the cracker.

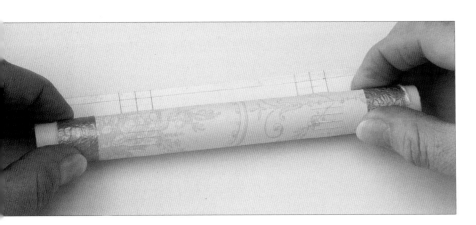

6. Apply a glue line to one edge of the back of the paper. Place the tube along the opposite edge and roll the paper round the tube.

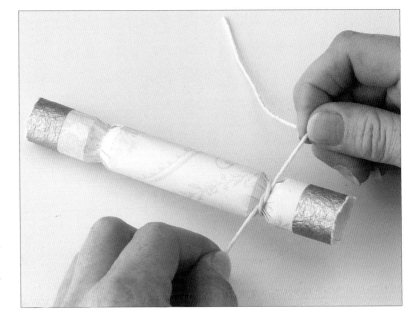

7. Remove the tube. Wrap a length of string around the middle scored line at one end of the cracker and pull to tighten. Repeat with the other end of the cracker.

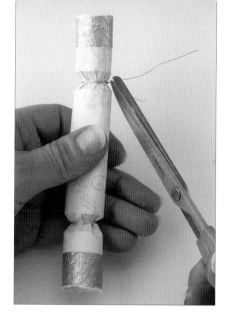

8. Remove the string and wrap the indentations with wire. Twist the ends of the wires together to secure and trim to neaten.

9. Cut a 5.5 x 7cm (2 x 2¾in) piece of gold paper and tear 5mm (¼in) from each edge. Use spray glue to attach it to the barrel of the cracker.

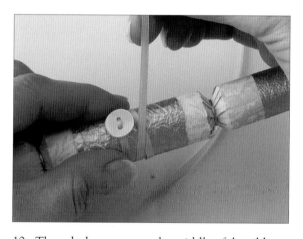

10. Thread a button on to the middle of the ribbon and wrap the ribbon around the cracker.

11. Tie the ribbon in a bow and trim the ends to neaten.

Using pastel coloured backing paper to create the cracker gives it a Victorian feel.

Opposite
Sprinkle your tree with
assorted crackers created with
different backing papers and
embellishments.

Star of Wonder

You will need:

A4 sheet of heavy watercolour paper

Coloured inks: magenta, cyan and violet

Star rubber stamp

Clear embossing pad

Gold embossing powder

Paintbrush

Gold card, 14cm x 14cm (5½ x 5½in)

Gold wire

Eyelet kit and hammer

Six gold eyelets

Black felt tip pen

Spray glue

Scalpel and cutting mat

Old scissors

Hairdryer

Heating tool

If, like me, you love playing and experimenting with colour and texture, then this project is for you. Have fun merging the coloured inks on watercolour paper to create your basic star. Then let fly with the stamp and embossing powder before lacing your star with wire for that final flourish.

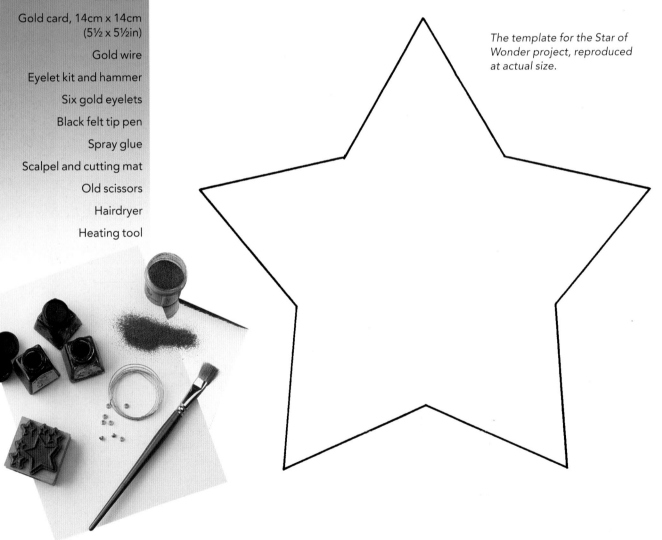

The template for the Star of Wonder project, reproduced at actual size.

1. Draw a 13cm (5in) square on to the middle of a piece of watercolour paper and paint it generously with water.

2. Spot the square with the magenta ink, letting the colour bleed across the damp surface.

3. While the square is still damp, spot the other inks on to the paper, letting them blend into each other until the whole surface is covered.

Tip
You can use a hairdryer to speed up the drying process.

4. Allow to dry. Press the star stamp into a clear embossing pad and stamp all over the square.

5. Sprinkle the square with embossing powder.

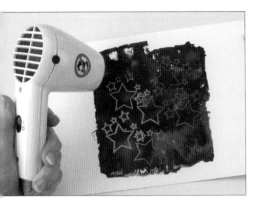

6. Shake off the excess powder and heat with a heating tool.

7. Photocopy and cut out the star template. Lay it on the painted square and draw round it with a felt tip pen. Cut it out.

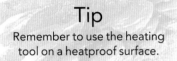

Tip
Remember to use the heating tool on a heatproof surface.

8. Spray glue the star to gold card and cut round it, leaving a small gold border.

9. Punch five holes round the inner points of the star and one at the top of the star.

10. Insert gold eyelets into the holes, turn the star over and hammer each eyelet with the setting tool.

11. Bring the wire up through one of the inner point eyelets, and working clockwise, take it down two eyelets further on. Still working clockwise, bring the wire up one eyelet further on, as shown.

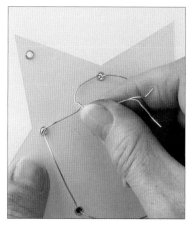

12. Continue threading the wire until you have a wire star on the front as shown. The wire should form a pentagon shape on the back of the star.

13. Twist the ends of the wire together at the back and trim.

14. Thread the top hole with wire, and spiral the wire ends around a paintbrush.

15. Finally, twist the wire ends together to create the hanger.

The pink and blue colouring of this decoration stands out well from the dark green foliage.

Emboss your basic stars with different stamps and powders and try lacing them with ribbons.

GLITZY GIFT BOX

You will need:

Papier-mâché box

White acrylic paint

Sheet of gold craft stickers

Sponge

Palette

Needle

White embroidery thread

Decorative large gold sequin

Gold beads

Faceted craft jewels

Ribbon, 70cm (27½in)

Clear glue

Scissors

Scalpel

These small papier-mâché boxes make unusual but attractive Christmas tree decorations. The box is sponged with acrylic paint to give an even, textured surface. A gift can be slipped into the box before assembling.

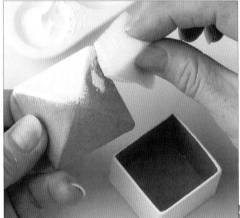

1. Sponge the lid and base of the box with white paint and leave to dry.

2. Apply a gold craft sticker to each facet of the lid.

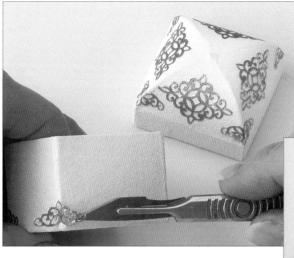

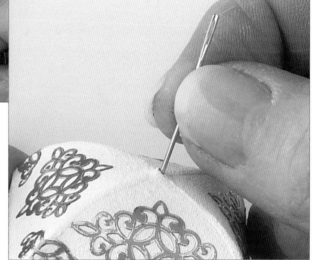

3. Apply the corner stickers to the lid and base.

4. Make a hole in the top of the lid with a needle.

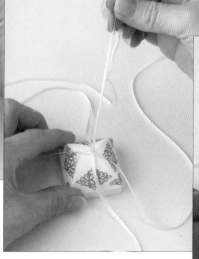

5. Thread the needle with two lengths of embroidery thread and knot the end. Push the needle up through the hole.

6. Thread it through the two lengths of ribbon.

7. Thread on the decorative sequin.

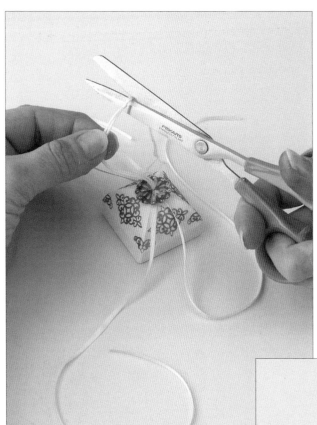

8. Remove the needle, tie the thread in a knot and trim the thread.

9. Insert your gift and put the lid on the base. Pull the ribbons down over the sides of the box and thread the ends through a bead.

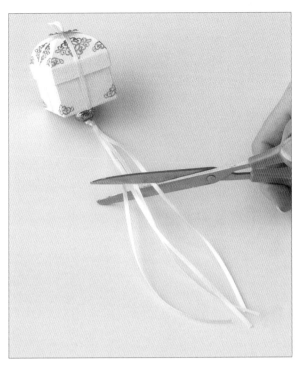

10. Tie a knot in the ribbons to secure the bead. Trim the ribbons.

11. Cut each ribbon lengthwise to create a tassel.

12. Glue a craft jewel to each facet of the lid.

These mini papier-mâché boxes are perfect for decorating and hanging on your tree.

Paint your boxes with traditional or funky colours – the choice is yours!

Templates

Use the alphabet templates and the heart and star templates for the Labels of Love project on pages 70–75. The heart, star and triangle templates can also be used to make Christmas tree garlands, following the instructions on pages 58–63.

These card angels are easy to make and fun to do. Use different coloured card for each angel to really make them stand out against the branches of your Christmas tree.

Decorate papier-mâché gift boxes with paint, stickers and jewels to make an extra-special tree gift.

Making Christmas Table Decorations

by Polly Pinder

Many of our Christmas traditions were introduced from Northern Europe during the Victorian era; but I have a feeling that in the darker days before Christmas was celebrated, our ancestors used flowers, leaves and other natural objects to decorate the table for a feast.

Planning the table for various festive meals is the perfect antidote to midwinter blues. Even if things are left to the last minute, there are always simple ideas which can be put together using a few craft items and an assortment of things found around the house. Many of the following designs evolved around bits and pieces from the previous year's cards and gift wrap. Do save anything that might have possibilities; your imagination can start working at the mere glimpse of any lovely shiny or shimmering thing.

The decorations in this section will brighten up the seasonal table and give some extra delight to family and friends. So, have a wonderful and memorable Christmas.

Polly

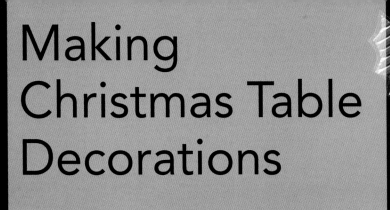

Materials

Paper

We really need to thank the producers of paper and card in the craft industry because every year they make available more exciting and sumptuous ranges for our little collections. We can dip into these, experiment with them and use our imaginations to create really beautiful objects. Here are many of the papers used in the following chapters. They include: red, green, gold and silver **self-adhesive holographic paper**; red and green **tissue paper**; **card**, silver **corrugated card** and **glitter card**; **synthetic copper-coloured spun paper**; **banana-leaf handmade paper**; gold and silver **metallic paper**; **strong, matt gold paper**; **scrap paper** to protect your work surface from spray paint and **tracing paper** for transferring designs. The one at the bottom is **draft film**. This can be bought at most art shops and is a perfect medium for diffusing candle light. I have used it for the candle shades on pages 104 to 109.

Beads and wire

Many craft shops now stock varieties of stunning **beads**. They come in so many shapes, sizes, colours and textures; and are made from different materials – glass, paper, wood, plastic and resin; some even have specks of gold flake embedded in them.

Companies are also producing different colours and thicknesses of **wire** for our crafts; I can remember having to use fuse wire not so long ago. **Florist's metal ribbon** is very malleable; I have used it to make a bow and tube cover on page 115. I found the **perforated metal sheeting** in a skip. It is used in radiator covers and can be bought from most hardware stores. It is surprisingly easy to cut with a pair of old scissors.

Headpins are long, blunt pins used in the jewellery industry. You will be able to get them from most bead shops.

Embellishments

All sorts of things can be used to embellish your Christmas table decorations. Lovely **ribbons** and **bows**, metallic and decorative **threads**; **gold-painted berries** and **pine cones**; **wire mesh hearts**, often woven with combinations of very narrow ribbon and sparkling seed beads; pieces cut from the stems of **artificial flowers**; coloured **feathers**, **string**, **packing straw** and **pipe cleaners**. In the spirit of recycling, do not forget the little things which adorned last year's presents and crackers; they can easily be adapted and enhanced to make new embellishments for this year.

Blanks

These are the objects used in the book as a basis for the decorations. Some of them can be found in most kitchens: various sized glasses, tea lights, loose bases from cake tins (not illustrated but used for the candle holder on page 126) and in the garden shed, little galvanised buckets and plant pots. The small gift bags and covered or blank boxes can be bought from craft shops and some stationers. The gold, red and blue candles are in most stores at this time of the year. Gold crockery is becoming increasingly popular. The lovely, large resin plates are often used as place mats and there are lots of ceramic dishes and bowls, one of which I have used as a stand for the centrepiece on page 115. This little wreath was bought at my local craft store. I pressed it down to form a flatter base for the Copper Trees Centrepiece on page 113. I found a set of the 'larger than usual' cork drinks mats in one of those wonderful stores which sell lots of unrelated things very cheaply. They had cartoon characters on the other side but they did not show with the mats turned upside down.

Other equipment

It really is easy and preferable to use a **cutting mat** when using your **metal ruler** and **craft knife**. It should last for years and no matter how much pressure you exert, the mat will heal up again. Do not forget to use your metal ruler when cutting, as a plastic one will not last long once the blade has nicked into it. A **plastic ruler** can be used for measuring.

You will also need an HB **pencil**, an **eraser** and a **black felt pen** for the Twirling Holly Candle Holder project on page 122.

You will need a few pairs of **scissors**: one or two pairs of fairly small, good quality sharp, pointed ones; a pair of deckle-edged for cutting snowflakes and an old pair for cutting thin wire. The **wire cutters** are needed for cutting any thick wire and the little **round-nosed pliers** are useful for bending and curling the wire.

I have used three kinds of sewing needle for the various materials (see the list at the beginning of each project): a **tapestry needle**, which has a blunt end; a **darning needle**, which is strong, long and sharp; and a **beading needle** which is very fine and sharp. A **thimble** is useful for pushing the fine beading needle through stiff card, as in the Copper Trees Centrepiece project on page 110. The **drinking straws** are used as tree trunks for the same project.

Glue is one of the most important items in the crafter's cupboard. I have used a **glue stick**, **clear all-purpose adhesive**, **sticky tape** and **double-sided tape** in three different widths. The **stapler** comes in handy when glue or tape are not strong enough.

Craft punches and an ordinary **office hole punch** are used in three of the projects and in many of the other decorations shown.

The **rubber stamps**, **inkpad** and **glitter** were used for the Simple Stamped Bags shown on page 121.

Nail varnish, particularly the pearlescent type, is really good for radically changing the appearance of a project. **Acrylic paint**, which becomes waterproof when dry, is equally useful. Always rinse your **paintbrushes** thoroughly when using the paint.

Craft stickers and **invisible thread** were used to make the Crystal Stars Candle Shade on page 109.

Fine horticultural **sand** can be bought from most garden centres. I have used it to secure things which need to stand upright in containers.

Gold and silver **spray paints** are used to decorate projects. The **decorating mask** is important and should always be worn while spraying, near an open window or door if possible.

Opposite
Gold and silver spray paint and a decorating mask; office hole punch; stapler; craft punches; clear all-purpose glue and glue stick; metal and plastic rulers; drinking straws; deckle-edged, ordinary, sharp, pointed and old scissors; wire cutters and round-nosed pliers; invisible thread, tapestry, darning and beading needles and a thimble; craft knife and cutting mat; paintbrushes, pencil and felt-tipped pen; eraser; craft stickers; double-sided tape in different widths; glitter; sticky tape; rubber stamps and inkpad; acrylic paint; nail varnish and sand.

CHRISTMAS CANDLE SHADE

You will need:

Brass coloured perforated metal sheeting 100 x 235mm (4 x 9¼in)

Bobbin of fine gold-coloured wire and tapestry needle

Old scissors, sharp-pointed scissors, craft knife and cutting mat

A4 sheet each of red and green self-adhesive holographic paper

Gold berry and leaf decoration on wire

A4 sheet each of red and green tissue paper

Draft film, 100 x 205mm (4 x 8in)

Small straight-sided glass tumbler, 60mm (2½in) in diameter and 85mm (3¼in) tall

Tea lights

Metal ruler and pencil

Sticky tape and glue stick

Decorative shades are a lovely way of enhancing ordinary tea lights. Each tea light is placed in a glass tumbler, then the tumbler is put into a decorated or perforated tube from which limited light is emitted. The outer form of this candle shade project is perforated metal sheeting, which I found in a skip – it had been used as a radiator cover. You can buy it in hardware stores, and it is soft enough to cut with old scissors. The little gold berries were bought as a larger bunch from my local craft shop, as were the holographic papers. The measurements here are dependent on the size of your tumbler. Remember that you must never leave a candle unattended.

1. Using your craft knife and metal ruler, cut the red and green tissue paper into 5 x 130mm (¼ x 5in) strips. Using the glue stick, stick the strips firmly on to the draft film, leaving a 5mm (¼in) gap between each strip. Trim the edges flush with the film.

2.   Attach half the width of a length of sticky tape along one edge (on the side where the strips have not been stuck). Bring the other edge round and press it on to the other half of the sticky tape, so that the tube is joined from the inside.

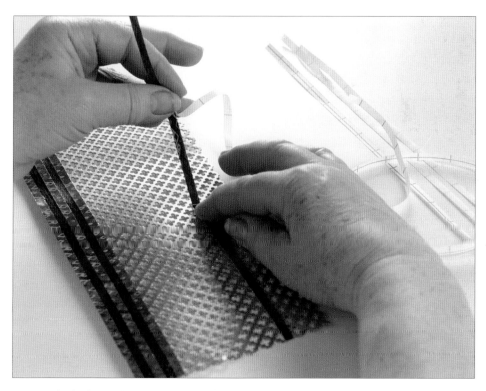

3.   Cut the holographic paper into six lengths, three of each colour, measuring 5 x 235mm (¼ x 9¼in). Peel off the backing and stick five round the base of the metal and one near the top at the same height as the glass tumbler.

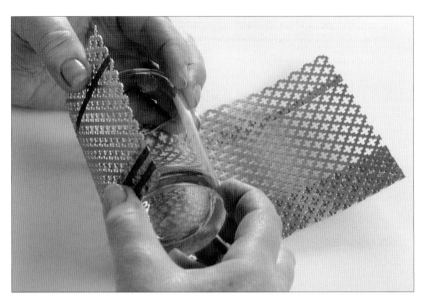

4. Curl the metal round the glass; this will help to achieve the tubular shape.

5. Overlap the edges by 10mm (½in) and neatly sew them together using a tapestry needle to thread the wire in and out of the perforations. Temporarily lift the strips of holographic paper so that you can reach the perforations on the top overlap.

6. Carefully thread the berry sprays into the perforations, pushing the wire stem in through the front, then out, then back in again. Press the wire stem against the inside of the shade.

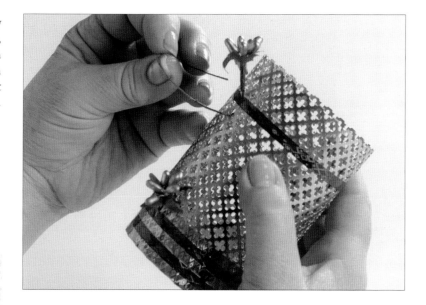

Tip

Be careful how you pick up the candle shade. Hold on to the bottom of the tumbler or it will fall out of the shade.

7. Slide the striped draft film liner inside the metal shade, seam against seam, being careful not to catch it on the wire stems. Carefully put the glass tumbler containing the candle inside the completed shade.

Tip

It is usually difficult to light the candle while it is in the tumbler. So, light the candle first, pinch the side of the candle's metal container with your pliers and carefully place it in the tumbler.

The finished candle shade. Light is magical, especially when it is reflected on shiny surfaces or transformed into rays coming from tiny apertures. These decorations will add a warm glow to the Christmas table.

Real Snowflakes and Crystal Stars

The images on the green candle shades are taken from magnified photographs of real snowflakes, which you can scan from this book (see page 141). Draw the outline of your candle shade on the computer screen and place the scanned snowflakes, then you may want to change the background colour to one of your choice.

In the white draft film shade, the crystal beads reflect light coming through star apertures. Each aperture was made by positioning an outline sticker, then cutting away the film inside the star. The beads are held in place by short lengths of invisible nylon thread which are caught by craft sticker stars.

COPPER TREES
CENTREPIECE

You will need

Two A4 sheets of orange card

Two A4 sheets of synthetic copper-coloured spun paper

A5 sheet of green glitter card

Various green and copper-coloured beads

Copper-coloured sewing thread, a beading needle and thimble

Wreath approximately 180mm (7in) in diameter

Three plant pots approximately 50mm (2in) in diameter across the top and fine sand to fill them

Green acrylic paint and paintbrush

Three green drinking straws

Circular cork mat or thick card 140mm (5½in) in diameter

Sharp-pointed scissors, craft knife, cutting mat and metal ruler

Double-sided tape, sticky tape and stapler

Tracing paper and pencil

Appreciative comments about the beautiful centrepiece, together with a glass of mulled wine, are always a good start to the Christmas meal. The trees for this project are made from orange card covered with a synthetic paper which has a look of finely spun frosted silk. It can be bought, together with the card, wreath and miniature plant pots, from most craft shops. I bought the cork mat from a hardware store but you could use a piece of sturdy card – just draw round a dish. Wonderful beads of all sizes, shapes and colours are available from specialist shops and mail order stockists.

1. Transfer the tree shape and circle on page 140 on to the orange card three times. Cut them out. Attach pieces of double-sided tape to the flaps on the circles, then use your craft knife to cut the central holes. Bend all the flaps down.

110

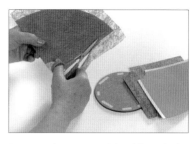

2. Attach pieces of double-sided tape down the sides of each tree shape. Press spun paper on top and then cut away the excess paper. Put pieces of double-sided tape round the edges of the cork mat, attach the spun paper and trim away the edges.

3. Use the copper-coloured thread and beading needle to sew beads on to the tree shape randomly, including strands of little seed beads. Knot each bead or strand securely at the back before going on to the next one. If you do not knot each bead at the back, when the shape is curled into a tree, the thread will becomes loose and the beads will dangle.

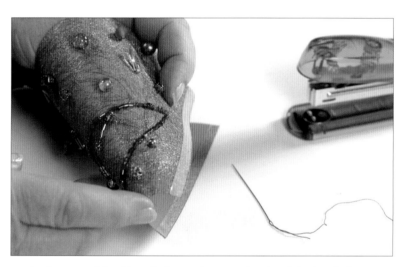

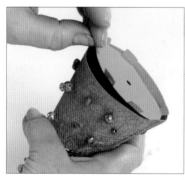

5. Remove the backing from the double-sided tape on the tabs around each circle. Place a circle inside the base of each tree shape and press the tabs to secure them.

4. Stick strips of double-sided tape down each side of the beaded shapes, one at the back and one at the front. Remove the backing and carefully curl the shape round, sticking the two sides together. Secure with a couple of stitches at the top and staples in the middle and at the bottom of the seam.

6. Place a piece of double-sided tape in the bottom of each pot. Give each pot two coats of green acrylic paint. Wash your brush immediately because acrylic paint dries hard very quickly.

7. Make four 20mm (¾in) slits at the bottom of a drinking straw and press the cut pieces outwards. Position the splayed ends on to the double-sided tape in a plant pot and pour sand up to the rim. Repeat with the other plant pots.

8. Cut nine strips of double-sided tape 5 x 25mm (¼ x 1in) and three 5 x 50mm (¼ x 2in). Position three small ones, crossing each other, on the top of each tree to cover the hole. Remove the backing after positioning each one. Stick the three longer pieces round the top edge.

9. Transfer the small star on page 140 on to the back of the glitter card twelve times. Cut the stars out and bend the points upwards. Turn them over and attach a piece of double-sided tape to one point of each star. Remove the backing and stick four sides together.

Tip

When you need to transfer an image many times (the twelve stars for example) it is easier to transfer one on to a piece of card, cut it out and then carefully draw round it twelve times.

10. Slide the trees on to the straws in the pots.

11. Carefully position the stars on top. Flatten the wreath to accommodate the mat then place the three pots on top. The wreath, mat and pots could be permanently attached using clear all-purpose glue if you wish.

Opposite

The finished centrepiece. Time is needed to make these little trees but you could always listen to a good Christmas play while sewing on the gorgeous beads. The spun paper is very easy to work with and has a stunning effect.

Shimmering Tree Centrepiece

This tree goes with the woven napkin rings on page 128. The weaving is stuck to the tube from a roll of cling film. The tree is made from two bunches of gold wire which I bought from one of those great shops that sell everything for virtually nothing. I made the gold stars, threaded some seed beads, punched out snowflakes and hung some little jewels and baubles.

All Wired Up Centrepiece

I bought two rolls of this wonderful wire at my local florist, where it is sold as florist's metal ribbon. The container is a cocoa tin covered with pearlescent paper and then the wire. The feathers, berries and gold cones were bought at a craft shop and having folded the wire up to make a ribbon bow, I filled the tin with sand, put everything in, then stood it on a little gold plate.

COUNTRY CARRIER GIFT BAG

You will need:

A4 sheet of textured handmade paper

Seven 250mm (10in) strands of rough string

A tiny spray of artificial berries

An artificial holly leaf

Fine packing straw

Craft knife, metal ruler and cutting mat

Double-sided tape

Scissors

Office hole punch

Tracing paper and pencil

These little bags can contain any lovely delight, perhaps a small, personal gift for each guest. The bags can be bought at most craft stores and some greetings card shops. They can be decorated using stamped images or spirelli designs (see pages 120–121), quilled shapes, beading or even stars and snowflakes punched from last year's Christmas cards.

It is not difficult to make little bags yourself – there is a template on page 139. I have chosen a heavily textured banana-leaf handmade paper which, combined with the string and packing straw, give a natural, country look. If you can not find artificial holly leaves, you can always cut one from some stiff green paper, using the template on page 139.

1. Transfer the bag template on to the back of your paper. Cut it out and indent the fold lines using the handle of your craft knife.

2. Fold all the creases, starting with the top narrow flap. Slide the folded top into the hole punch and make the four holes where indicated.

3. Attach pieces of double-sided tape to the two larger flaps and to the back of the side flap as shown. Peel off the backing.

4. First stick the two sides together with the flap inside. Then tuck the small bottom flaps in and stick the larger ones on top. Press from the inside to ensure a firm attachment.

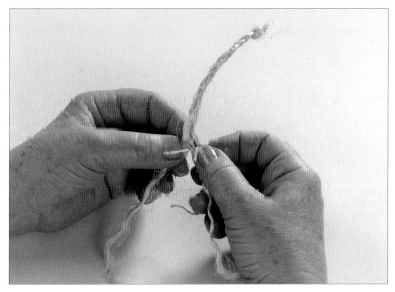

5. Knot three strands of string together and plait them firmly.

6. Thread the plait through two holes on one side of the bag, then knot the ends on the inside of the bag. Make another plait with three more strands and attach it in the same way.

7. Wind the remaining strand into a flat circle. Carefully, without allowing it to spring away, press it on to a piece of double-sided tape. Trim off any excess tape.

8. Remove the backing from the wound string and attach the berry spray and holly leaf behind the string. Put another piece of double-sided tape behind all three items and press it securely on to the bag.

9. Place a handful of packing straw into the bag, together with the chosen gift.

Tip

You could use a tiny spray of fresh red berries and a real holly leaf, or perhaps variegated ivy instead of holly to avoid injury.

Opposite
These little gift bags are really easy to make. I have used a highly textured, handmade banana-leaf paper, but an ordinary strong, brown wrapping paper would look just as good. I have put two stitches through the tops of the handles to keep them together, but this is unnecessary if you feel that your guest will want quick access to the contents!

Spirelli Snowflake Bags

Sometimes it is nice to deviate from the traditional Christmas colours and introduce something new, like this lovely purple holographic paper. The little snowflakes were cut with a craft punch from sparkly card. The large spirelli snowflake was cut out using deckle-edged scissors. Metallic purple thread was used to wind round the pieces of flake which were then stuck together.

Simple Stamped Bags

I bought these and the purple bags from a greetings card shop. The holographic papers are irresistible; they have such a magical effect, showing all the colours of the rainbow. The idea is to have a different Christmas image on each little bag. The image was stamped using silver sparkle embossing powder. The red pearlescent circles were cut from last year's Christmas carrier bag. I used two stitches to secure the little bow and the bag filling is red tissue paper.

TWIRLING HOLLY CANDLE HOLDER

You will need:

Galvanised bucket 80mm (3in) high and 90mm (3½in) in diameter, and fine sand to fill it

Red candle 100mm (4in) tall

Round red glass beads, red cotton thread and a needle

A5 sheet of corrugated silver card

A5 sheet of silver paper

A5 sheet of red self-adhesive holographic paper

Piece of plain card 80mm (3in) square

Roll of sturdy silver-coloured wire and wire cutters

Pencil, tracing paper and black felt pen

Small, sharp, pointed scissors

Double-sided tape

Although candles are used more frequently now, as an aid to relaxation and to create a romantic atmosphere, there is still a particular magic about the flickering light of a Christmas candle.

The decidedly unromantic galvanised bucket used for this project was found gathering dust and cobwebs in my greenhouse. It had been home to a cactus until the plant grew too large. I like the slight craziness of this concept – twirling holly, bouncing gently at the least movement; and lots of shiny red beads to suggest juicy berries. The narrow border of holographic paper round the leaves gives a wonderful sparkle when the candle is lit.

Do be sure that the leaves are all bending away from the candle flame and never leave any of the candles in this book unattended, particularly when there are children about.

1. Transfer the holly leaves on page 139 on to the piece of plain card. Cut them out to make templates. Lay the smallest one on the front of the corrugated card and, using the felt pen, draw round it seven times. It is easier to cut the holly if you first cut each one out roughly to separate it from the others. Cut the corrugated paper from the front. If you cut from the back, you will tear the silver on the front.

2. Remove the backing from the red holographic paper and stick the silver paper in its place, so that they are back to back. Lay the larger holly template on the silver side and draw round it seven times. Cut out each holly leaf, trying to cut within the black line.

3. Stick a piece of double-sided tape on the back of a corrugated leaf. Attach it to a red leaf. Stick another piece of tape on the back of the red leaf then stick it on the front of the bucket, at an angle as shown.

4. Using the wire cutters, cut six pieces of wire of varying lengths starting from 280mm (11in). Stick a piece of double-sided tape down the centre front of each red leaf, then down the centre back of each corrugated leaf.

5. Remove the backing and lay a piece of wire on the double-sided tape on a red leaf. Carefully lay the corrugated leaf on top and press together firmly. Repeat with the other leaves.

Tip
The wire used for making decorations is usually fairly soft; if you do not have wire cutters, you can use old scissors.

6. Thread three beads on to each wire. To make a spring, start 80mm (3in) from the end of the wire and wrap it smoothly round your thumb, but not too tightly. Slide the spring off your thumb: it can be now be stretched out or pushed tighter.

7. Pour sand into the bucket, leaving roughly a depth of one bead at the top. Push the candle firmly into the centre. Use the needle to thread enough beads onto the cotton to wind once round the base of the candle. Knot the cotton securely, then position the string of beads round the base. Put some loose beads on top to disturb the uniformity.

8. Push the holly springs into the sand and twist them carefully until the arrangement is balanced and to your liking. The springs can be removed and adjusted if required.

Opposite
The finished candle holder. The silver colour scheme creates a fresh, modern look and makes a change from the usual Christmas gold. The fine sand which supports the candle and springs can be bought from garden centres.

Snowflakes and Ice Cubes

I could not resist the magnificently detailed silver card that forms the curved part of this candle holder. I made a base from cardboard, covered it with silver paper, edged it with gold and added gold outline stickers. I backed the silver card with silver paper, then used double-sided tape to stick it on to the base – it curved naturally because the base width was narrower than the card. The silver backing paper reflects the gold outline stickers on the base. The glass cube candle holders are stuck on with clear all-purpose glue.

Opposite

Christmas Cocktails

I bought these cocktail glasses from a charity shop. Upside down, they make perfect holders for the square blue candles. The base is made from two baking tin bases, covered with metallic and holographic papers and stuck together with double-sided tape. The most difficult thing was trying to keep the metallic straw in the glasses – it has a mind of its own. Everything can be reclaimed after the festivities.

GOLDEN WEAVE NAPKIN RINGS

You will need:

To make one ring:

Strong, matt gold paper 50 x 180mm (2 x 7in)

Strips of gold paper, card, thread, cord, pipe cleaner and ribbon roughly 5 x 70mm (¼ x 2¾in)

Gold, self-adhesive holographic paper

Fine gold wire

Cardboard tube from a kitchen towel roll

Snowflake craft punch

Craft knife, scissors, old scissors for cutting wire and cutting mat

Double-sided tape and sticky tape

Pencil and metal ruler

Coordinating your table decorations creates a sense of visual unity and cohesion. These woven napkin rings go with the Shimmering Tree Centrepiece on page 114. In order to achieve the lovely golden weave, I gathered together absolutely anything that had a hint of gold – old greeting cards and Christmas crackers, pipe cleaners, thread, cord, ribbon, holographic paper and bits of packaging. The main part of the ring is made from a sturdy matt gold paper. The ends of each threaded strip are cut obliquely, or cut and curled, or frayed. It is lovely to watch the different golden textures and shades grow as you weave them through.

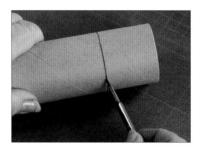

1. Using your pencil and ruler, measure and draw a line round the tube 45mm (1¾in) from the edge. Then, using your craft knife and a sawing motion, cut the section off.

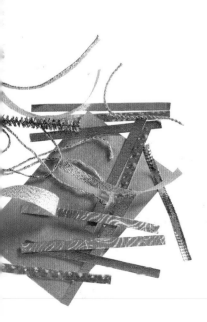

Tip
If you have found some interesting gold paper which is too flimsy to use either as the ring or the strips, simply stick some ordinary cartridge or typing paper on the back to make it firmer.

2. Turn the matt gold paper over. Draw lines 20mm (¾in) from the top and bottom edges. Then draw nine lines 5mm (³⁄₁₆in) apart between the top and bottom lines. Carefully cut along the vertical lines.

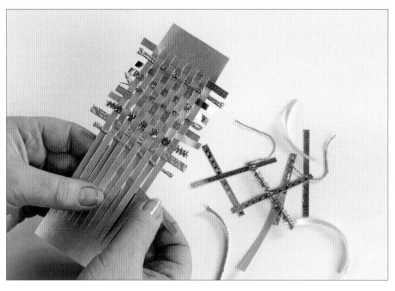

3. Start to thread the various strips of gold alternately through the matt gold bands.

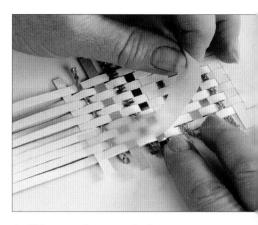

4. When you have reached half way, turn the weaving over. Firmly push each side in so that all the bands are as close as possible. Secure each side with a piece of sticky tape. Continue threading, then tighten and secure the remaining half in the same way.

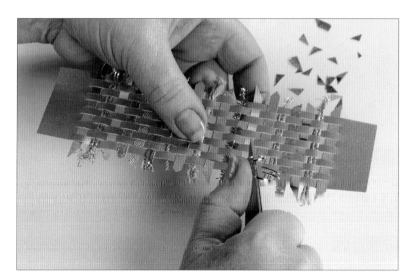

5. With the front of the weaving facing you, cut some of the strip ends diagonally or to a point, curl others round your scissors as shown and fray the ends of any cord or ribbon.

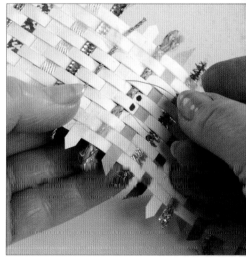

6. Using the old scissors, cut three pieces of wire 90mm (3½in) long. Mark the centre of the weaving on the back then thread each wire through so that both ends stick out of the front. Secure the wires at the back with a piece of sticky tape.

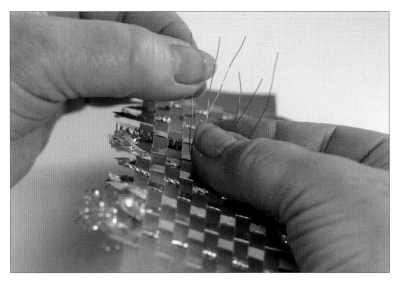

7. Straighten the wires at the front so that they stand up as shown.

8. Attach a piece of double-sided tape round the centre of the cardboard tube. Then attach another piece to the top back border of the weaving. Carefully but firmly wrap the weaving round the tube. The weaving should overlap the tube slightly at both sides.

9. Punch twelve snowflakes from the gold holographic paper. Remove the backing and using the tip of your craft knife, carefully attach two snowflakes, sticky side to sticky side, to the tip of each wire.

Opposite
The finished napkin rings. These richly woven decorations can be used at the table together with the matching Shimmering Tree Centrepiece (page 114).

Classical Holly Napkin Rings

Here I chose red and green glitter card and a stiff, textured paper, the same colour as the napkins. A single craft punch combined the holly with a decorative border and an office hole punch made the gold and silver holographic circles and the holes through which the metallic ribbon was threaded.

Beads and Berries Napkin Rings

*These were so simple to make. I used last year's Christmas crackers to make the
box-like ring, then strung all the varying sized beads on thin wire, wrapped the
beaded wire round the rings, then wired the leaves and berries on to each end.*

STAR SHINE SURPRISE BOXES

These little boxes have the same function as the gift bags; they contain nice surprises for your Christmas guests. It is a good idea, if possible, to make them coordinate with other table decorations such as the centrepiece or napkin rings.

The blank boxes are usually a natural brown colour and need covering or painting. They come in several different shapes and are available from craft stores. I have used a star-shaped box for this project and sprayed the lid gold and the box silver. The rays of star shine are headpins, which you can buy from most bead shops, with tiny beads threaded on.

You will need:

To make one box:

Star-shaped blank box

Gold and silver spray paint, mask and scrap paper

Gold and silver seed beads

Fifteen silver wire headpins and 150mm (6in) of silver wire

Silver glitter card, 80 x 130mm (3 x 5in)

Sheet each of self-adhesive gold and silver metallic paper, 50 x100mm (2 x 4in)

Scissors, craft knife and cutting mat

Tracing paper, pencil and metal ruler

Small and medium star craft punches

Double-sided tape, sticky tape and clear all-purpose glue

Little paintbrush or wooden skewer

Round-nosed pliers, wire cutters and darning needle

1. Cover your working surface with scrap paper to protect it, put your mask on and open a window. Position the box and lid then spray the box silver and the lid gold.

2. When the box and lid are dry, punch out approximately ten medium and ten small gold stars, then thirteen medium and eighteen small silver stars from the self-adhesive paper. Remove the backing with the tip of your craft knife and stick the gold stars on the box and the silver stars on the lid.

3. Transfer the large star on page 141 on to the back of the glitter card, twice. Cut the stars out using your craft knife, ruler and cutting mat or sharp, pointed scissors. Using the knife, cut a 5mm (¼in) hole in the centre of one star.

4. Stick a small piece of double-sided tape on to the back of the leftover glitter card, then punch out a small star. Position a medium gold star and the small glitter star in the centre of the other large star.

5. Wind the wire round the paintbrush handle to make a spring. Pull a little of the end out and attach it to the centre underside of the large glitter star without a hole, using a piece of double-sided tape. Add a piece of sticky tape to secure it firmly.

6. Thread ten mixed beads each on to two headpins and fourteen on to another. Position the headpin with most beads in the centre then use your round-nosed pliers to hold the pins and twist tightly so that the three are held together. Repeat four more times so that you have a total of five star shine rays.

7. Using the wire cutters, cut the ends from each of the five beaded rays, leaving about 5mm (¼in) of twisted pins.

8. Place the rays round the spring as shown. Attach them using double-sided tape underneath and sticky tape on top, as for the spring.

9. Lay the completed star face down, squeeze a little clear glue round the centre then slide the other glitter star face down over the spring. Position it firmly making sure that the star points correspond with the beaded rays.

10. When the glue is completely dry, place a piece of double-sided tape on the inside centre of the box lid. Use the darning needle to pierce a hole in the centre. Push the end of the spring through and press it on to the double-sided tape, then cover it with sticky tape to secure it.

Opposite

The finished boxes. There is something undeniably cheeky about things wobbling on a little spring. This gorgeous star is attached to a handmade spring and vibrates gently at the slightest movement. I am going to use these Star Shine Surprise Boxes for a special Christmas Eve dinner party and put a delicious home-made chocolate in each one.

Yuletide Love Boxes

These are flat-pack boxes that you can buy from greetings card shops and stationers. I used invisible thread to sew the lovely mixed beads to the wire mesh hearts and stuck the hearts on to the boxes with clear all-purpose glue. The folded ribbon is secured in place with double-sided tape and a tiny punched heart has been stuck to the flat part of the ribbon, emphasising the love theme.

Templates

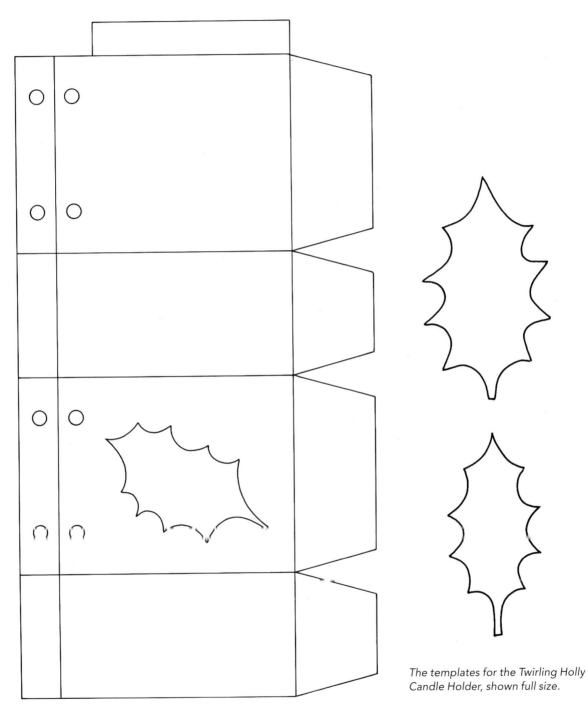

The template for the Country Carrier Gift Bag, shown at seventy-five per cent of actual size. Enlarge it to 133 per cent on a photocopier.

The templates for the Twirling Holly Candle Holder, shown full size.

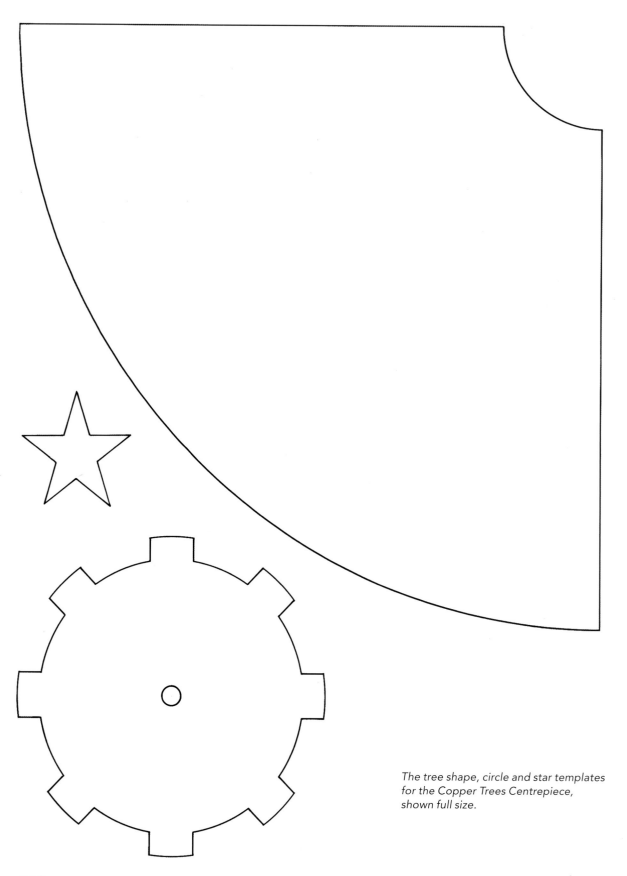

The tree shape, circle and star templates
for the Copper Trees Centrepiece,
shown full size.

These photographs of real snowflakes can be scanned from this page and used to make the snowflake candle shades shown on page 109.

The template for the Star Shine Surprise Box, shown full size.

Mix and Match Gift Boxes

I have decorated these to show how useful it is to keep bits and pieces. The embellishments were collected from last year's Christmas crackers. The gift boxes have been transformed by the addition of gold foliage, green holographic paper, matt gold paper and plum-coloured nail varnish applied to the pearls and diamond settings.

Opposite

Handmade decorations make the Christmas table really special.

Index